Tipton Poetry Journal – Spring 2020

Tipton Poetry Journal, located in the heartland of the Midwest, publishes quality poetry from Indiana and around the world.

This issue features 50 poets from the United States (20 different states) and 4 poets from Canada, Spain and the United Kingdom.

This issue was assembled as the COVID-19 pandemic was gathering strength in the United States and around the world. A few of the poems reflect this, beginning with the opening "Quarantine" by Anannya Uberoi. Doris Lynch composed "Nestbuilding in a A Difficult Season" and Rosaleen Crowley offers "reflections on then and now." We close the issue with Marjie Giffin's "Empty City." Hopefully, our cover photo of a chamomile daisy breaking through cobblestones also evokes for others the hope of a single flower blooming in an empty, pandemic world.

Cover Photo: "Single chamomile breaking through cobbles" by MaxManin. Licensed Shutterstock Image #1114592360. http://shutterstock.com/g/MaxManin

Print versions of *Tipton Poetry Journal* are available for purchase through amazon.com.

Barry Harris, Editor

Copyright 2020 by the Tipton Poetry Journal.

All rights remain the exclusive property of the individual contributors and may not be used without their permission.

Tipton Poetry Journal is published by Brick Street Poetry Inc., a tax-exempt non-profit organization under IRS Code 501(c)(3). Brick Street Poetry Inc. publishes the Tipton Poetry Journal, hosts the monthly poetry series *Poetry on Brick Street* and sponsors other poetry-related events.

Tipton Poetry Journal – Spring 2020

Contents

Anannya Uberoi 1
Mark Vogel 2
F.X. James 3
Jessica Nguyen 4
Karla Linn Merrifield 5
Norbert Krapf 6
Bill Hollands 7
Fida Islaih 8
Donna Pucciani 10
Rosaleen Crowley 11
Craig McVay 12
Alex Pickens 13
Mary Birnbaum 14
Blair Benjamin 16
Jan Ball 18
Patrick Kalahar 19
Hadley Austin 20
D.R. James 24
Philip C. Kolin 26
Lylanne Musselman 27
Timothy Robbins 28
Timothy Pilgrim 29
Ron Riekki 30
William Pruitt 30
Vivian Wagner 32
Bruce Levine 33

Tipton Poetry Journal – Spring 2020

James Mulhern 34
Michael Chang 35
Michael Brockley 36
Mary Hills Kuck 38
Douglas Cole..39
Patrick Theron Erickson 40
Doris Lynch..41
James Green 42
Daniel Edward Moore 43
Barry Peters 44
Richard Dinges, Jr. 46
Casey Killingsworth...47
J.P. Check 48
Duane Anderson 49
Wally Swist 50
Nathaniel Dolton-Thornton..51
William Snyder, Jr. 52
Danielle Wong 53
Gabriel Welsch 54
Katie Richards...55
J.J. Steinfeld..56
Glen Armstrong...57
Lois Marie Harrod 58
Renee Emerson..59
Marjie Giffin 60
Contributor Biographies 62

Tipton Poetry Journal – Spring 2020

Quarantine
Anannya Uberoi

I arrived at work, ten-ish, to pack up, and something
was off. The blinds were up, my desk looking outward to

a bright, sunny day – did this world really exist in front
of my office window, and how? I gently let my attention

rivet to the romanesque building outside the window
beyond the two-headed giant of a screen in front of me,

the big gabled roof articled to the upright sky, a small
gathering of gifts, a weather doll hanging to the left

of a jemmied front door, some mother screaming, her
yellowing plants setting aside one particular house

from the unicolored building – nothing chromatic,
a dulled down shade of brick red lined by white,

delicate white curtains responding to the hefty wind,
the rooftop balcony canopy fanning the entire building

in a kingdom full of owners. Biforate, safe, quarantined
space created under urban skies, and once more I sat

engaged and secured to my seat, my soul growing
silent as a leafless tree against the sepia sky.

Backyards, town halls, lofts, back to their still, unmoving
states. Mothers knitting, children sleeping, cities ducked

in a silence of moons and moons of winter.
'Safe!' chuckled I, 'yes, safe.'

Anannya Uberoi is a full-time software engineer and part-time tea connoisseur based in Madrid. Her poems and short stories have appeared or are forthcoming in *Jaggery, LandLocked, Deep Wild, Lapiz Lazuli,* and *eFiction India*. Her writing has also been featured on *The Delhi Walla* and *The Dewdrop*, among other literary blogs.

the bait is taken
Mark Vogel

How shocking that those in charge haven't mustered
sufficient energy to fully poison the St. John's River
weaving through Jacksonville, though many
clearly worked hard to channel the big and deep
thriving beneath the glittering surface.

In this liquid dawn just emerging from the dark,
already a significant banging drifts over the water
as the great shipyard gains momentum. A Navy
helicopter unbelievably comes in low, saying
the many humans here are awake, and continue

to do what they desire, oblivious to one skinny tourist
standing on a private dock with a borrowed pole,
barely understanding the whole inner coastal concept.
This visitor nonetheless absurdly flings a frozen
shrimp far out into the green blue swirl, nothing

like home's clear rushing mountain streams. Soon
enough a maybe-imagined pull is followed quick
with a powerful yank. And then, before this premonition
of *Maybe* can take form, a steady pull says unseen
proof exists that a big creature lives and turns

and moves, caught on my line, that currents and
connections have always existed bigger than me.
Then just as quick the line is lifeless, the heart-pumping
promise melted away, leaving only a vision now
in doubt, still believing something huge has

brushed close. Then a bit of sun hits the surface,
and a hundred feet out a three-foot tail breaks
the surface, as if just for me. Then just as quick,
the evidence disappears in moving water no human
eyes could plumb. Then, again the lonely tableau,

like the too-familiar human condition — a pathetic
visitor stands alone, comic, on the shifting dock,
alive to a twisted smile, struggling to understand.

Mark Vogel lives at the back of a Blue Ridge holler with his wife, Susan Weinberg, an accomplished fiction and creative non-fiction writer, and two foster sons. He currently serves as Professor of English at Appalachian State University in Boone, North Carolina, where he co-directs the English Education Program. Poems and short stories have appeared in several dozen literary journals.

saving

F.X. James

Somewhere, on an island off the coast of Norway, where there
is only ice and more ice to spare, they are saving seeds in a
subterranean vault: maize, wheat, rice, soy, cowpea, barley,
potato, etc. The idea is sound, for who knows what will soon
happen to us with our greedy abusive ways. Custodians
package the seeds in plastic boxes, then wheel them down
the chilly throat of ice and rock, to stack them on wooden
shelves like books, or like gifts insipid family members bring
from overseas, those poorly made ornaments from unpaved
South American villages: thickly painted donkeys that crumble
from the lightest touch, saints with asymmetrical hands pressed
palm to palm under miserable drooping faces. The custodians
smoke cigarettes during their breaks. They drink rich black
coffee from small plastic cups. Their world is ice and more
ice, and our future, grouped in small smooth dots in their
outstretched palms.

F. X. James is the pseudonym for an oddball British expat hiding out in Minnesota. When not dissolving in another savage summer or fattening up for the next brutal winter, he's writing poems and stories on the backs of unpaid utility bills, and drinking too much dark ale. His words have appeared in many a magazine, and on a lucid day he can see all sorts of crazy things.

The Little Crows
Jessica Nguyen

A murder of little
crows sat in. A line
next to me at a cafe

Delicate omens, treasuring
their moments among
the living —— zipping their espressos

(I thought)

Brushes with Death
poses them to be
The time keepers

(I thought)

Curiosity does not bring them back (like the cats)
Curiosity is what makes them black

But no,

They have simply
strayed too far
from the sun

Jessica Nguyen is a playwright, electronic musician, and writer living in Brooklyn. She has been published previously in *Tipton Poetry Journal, Open Thought Vortex, Sisyphus Quarterly, Crab Fat Magazine,* and *The Sex Letters Project.* She has also performed and written for The Boston Center for the Arts, The Living Gallery, Bindlestiff Studios, The Exponential Festival, and The Trans Theatre Festival.

Danse Nue
Karla Linn Merrifield

Under star-masked
mild midnight autumn sky
I dance on my suburban deck
al fresco   nude
railing mid-spine
slats pressing 'gainst my ass—
cricket skritch skritch—
I inch down their rhythm
muscle-deep yoga-chair pose
hips hips hips shift sway swing
scapulae against crossboard
femurs thrusting clouds

An electric candle flickers
light you know
off my elbow
out of reach
of arms flung
to Time's dry-leafed
season of thighs and crisp sighs

Karla Linn Merrifield has had 800+ poems appear in dozens of journals and anthologies. She has 14 books to her credit. Following her 2018 *Psyche's Scroll* (Poetry Box Select) is the new *Athabaskan Fractal: Poems of the Far North* from Cirque Press. She lives in Florida and is currently at work on a poetry collection, *My Body the Guitar*, inspired by famous guitarists and their guitars to be published by Before Your Quiet Eyes Holograph Series (Rochester, NY) in late 2021.

Crazy Horse Is One
Norbert Krapf

after Jody Naranjo, Santa Clara Pueblo Potter

He is one with his horse
at one with himself
and all generations.

He is inside, outside time
that is pure illusion
on a road that runs

in all directions
that leads into
vision from beyond

flowing into him
as his hair flows
out straight behind.

He is one, he is one
with himself
and his horse

and his vision
and the wind
and the sun

and the moon
and the stars
and night and day.

He is all eye
one with all that is
essence of motion

hurtling into spirit
into bright light
illuminating all.

Former Indiana Poet Laureate **Norbert Krapf** is the author of thirteen poetry collections, including the recent *Indiana Hill Country Poems*. Forthcoming is *Southwest by Midwest,* which includes "Crazy Horse Is One." He is the winner of a Glick Indiana Author Award, a Creative Renewal Fellowship from the Arts Council of Indianapolis, and the Lucille Medwick Memorial Award from the Poetry Society of America. He collaborates with bluesman Gordon Bonham.

Thief
Bill Hollands

Black wing-
tips, yours, mine
now. Two crows
curled, concealing
tongues. Waxy
laces worm
through eyelets. I
lift them from
their nest. My
gold toes offer
brief life.

Following a B.A. from Williams College, **Bill Hollands** received a Dr. Herchel Smith Fellowship for two years of graduate work at Cambridge University, where he received his M.A. in English. He worked as a librarian for The New York Public Library and published a professional trade book, *Teaching the Internet to Library Staff and Users*. He is now a public high school English teacher in Seattle, where he lives with his husband and son. Poems are forthcoming in *Crosswinds* and *PageBoy*.

Changing Landscape
Fida Islaih

Weekly bookstore dates
down on Mercantile
I can see for miles
cornfields and cows

watch the cityscape change
fields becoming neighborhoods
I went to school feeling misunderstood
a little mosque on the prairie
now sits by a church and Sikh temple

a golden dome shines
on the horizon
as we enjoy an interfaith feast
i'll try to change your outlook
it's time to accept the storyline.

Small Town Gems
Fida Islaih

I fix my headscarf in public
making eye contact
some people hurry away
while others share a smile

Driving around
a stranger gives a peace sign;
catch a glimpse of the sunset
in the rear view mirror
make a u-turn to follow it

Small town gems are
bumping into familiar faces
at the grocery store and we catch up
years of going to the same bookstore
and the barista knows me

It's hard to find the empty roads
lined with woods
but when I do
my heart grows
I can let the windows down
feel the wind
breathe the fresh air.

Fida Islaih is a self-published poet of seven collections and a freelance poetry editor living in Fishers, Indiana.

Disappearing Act
Donna Pucciani

The moon is melting
into dawn, her gibbous clarity
dissolving on one side,
the ice of an early frost
nibbling at her gleaming visage
like a rabbit's teeth on a cabbage.

This magic globe, mistress of the night,
used to be whole, her face turning
in the sky by another's light, rising
from myth and legend, lighting
the silhouette of a howling wolf,
spinning a tale of green cheese
to a child at bedtime.

Now it seems she dribbles down
like spilt milk, ready to vanish
into the cosmic cycle of tides.
She will not cease to exist,
but merely darken, her lunar body
no longer illumined but still alive
somewhere out there in a universe
whose arms have grown tired
of holding her.

Donna Pucciani, a Chicago-based writer, has published poetry worldwide in such diverse publications as *Shi Chao Poetry, Istanbul Literary Review, Poetry Salzburg, The Pedestal,* and *Journal of Italian Translation.* Her most recent book of poems is *EDGES.*

reflection on then and now
Rosaleen Crowley

then, I remember smell of coffee at Cafe Buondi,
lavender mimosa with smoked salmon at Patachou,
sound of laughter in a crowded room,
a bouncing ball at a volleyball game.

now, grateful for sounds that surround me,
dishwasher converts to sea splash,
silence has a vibrating sound in my ear,
grumbling stomach, never had time to hear that before.

looking in the pantry is like doing calculus
you know it has a meaning but not quite understood,
cans of beans, corn, mackerel and tomatoes,
packets of pasta, rice and wine.

coffee brewing leaves wafting aroma,
beef stew after five days has served us well,
chicken defrosting to change things up,
thirteen days on self isolation for two.

more staring at the closet, choosing clothes to wear,
wrapped in a scarf brings comfort,
wool, silk, cotton, winter and summer clothes together,
each day a different color combination to keep in style.

funny how smell is the first sense to come to mind
they say it is also among the last to leave.

Rosaleen Crowley was in born in Cork, Ireland and graduated from University College Cork. She relocated to Carmel, Indiana, in 1990. Along with images of water, nature and open spaces, themes of home, love, conflict, loss and isolation are looked at through her poetry. Her third book in her trilogy, *Point of Perception* will be published later this year.

The Poet Faces the Dawn
Craig McVay

Blind, she pulls on jeans and shirt as frozen
winds squeeze between the skinny brown slats
of the back door. She sees only the dark
meant for no one but her.

    She is alone, but for the ghosts of friends
    she no longer wishes to talk with. Invisible
    friends who coiled and struck at her because
    she told the truth.

She drinks the stink of the rusty water she pumped
last night and, with her brown knuckled hands,
washes the dishes from supper. Cold wind
smacks her back.

    She wishes the ghosts of her parents would
    come see her. Questions beg for answers.
    Why did they leave her with the ugly aunt?
    Why did they take her brother, but not her?

Craig McVay, originally from West Lafayette, Indiana, has lived with his wife —and family nearby— in Columbus, Ohio for most of the past forty years. His degrees are in English and Classics, both of which he has taught in schools, community colleges and prisons in Maryland and Central Ohio; he currently is teaching mythology for Columbus State Community College. Co-ordinator of the longtime Columbus reading series, Peripatetic Poets, he has stories and poems in *Avatar Review, Blue Uniorn, Common Threads, Grey Sparrow, Icon* and others. A chapbook, *Joy in the Tomb of Hunting and Fishing*, will be published this spring or summer.

"Alex"

Alex Pickens

I am a poem I composed in
the universe with my soul as the pen,
inscribed in space-time and then left for
my progeny and the world to find.

My childhood is a short stanza poorly
wrote, absurdist impressionism where
nothing makes sense and nothing rhymes
and life passes in irregular rhythms.

Parents protect me until my teens, when
comes that volta called *puberty*, and then
nothing is what I expect it to be
and I am seized by an urge to procreate.

But the lines, like the ones on my face,
multiply and spread across the page
because I don't know what to do when
I walk down the aisle with my best friend.

Soon this poem will have sequels and
metaphors, little boys and little girls
who expect me to tell them what to do,
not realizing that I still have no clue.

I suppose a poem this bad deserves
to be wadded up and thrown in the trash
but God saved this poem called "Alex"
on His wall, like something a child might draw.

Alex Pickens grew up in the Appalachian mountains between New England and Virginia. This year his poetry has been accepted by *Hawaii Pacific Review, Crab Orchard Review,* and *Constellations*, while last year his work was nominated for Best of the Net and a Pushcart Prize. He is the winner of *Appalachia journal's* 2019 Waterman Fund Essay Contest. Alex lives in North Carolina.

Origami Star
Mary Birnbaum

My origami breath folds & unfolds round me
fingers of light pointing to the next crease
the neat twinning of dimension
the fan of time snapping open its tiny breeze

the geology of sound suspends our bones
rose fascia coalesce cobweb stems all around
the red paper of butterflies
kisses air cluttered with the pulse of petals

the most extravagant gesture the million
leaves of a nova its epic a remote memory
visible as a winking out a tremor
I pressed this star clumsy between my fingertips

Neither Crying Nor Thinking
Mary Birnbaum

I was thinking about you and me,
because thinking is better than crying.

Consulting boxes full of shadow moths,
yellowing newspaper stories that fell in love
with yellow sun,
wrinkles that fell in gleaming love
with the prow of the iron.

But, no, it wasn't like that—
neither crying nor thinking.
Youth falls in love with youth,
lips borrow the softness of lips,
wounds cover wounds.

The tear in the pocket your life fell out of—
you never noticed what the sharp edge did.

Give it here, I'll mend it again,
clean it, order new curtains.
When night finally softens,
so will I. Waking in sorrow, helpless,
I open your familiar back.
I am persistent as breath. You turn,
my face climbs
to its old place on your shoulder.

Mary Birnbaum was born, raised, and educated in New York City. She has studied poetry at the Joiner Institute in UMass, Boston. Mary's translation of the Haitian poet Felix Morisseau-Leroy has been published in the *Massachusetts Review*, the anthology *Into English* (Graywolf Press), and will be in the 60 year anniversary anthology of the *Massachusetts Review* as well. Her work is forthcoming or has recently appeared in *I-70 Review, the J Journal,* and *Nixes Mate Review*.

I am using an example from everyday life because of your human limitations
Blair Benjamin

Romans 6:19

You know how when you're stocking shelves and sometimes
everything crashes down because a careless person

assembled the shelf, or made a flawed design.
Nothing in your programming could have averted the fall.

Or how when you vacuum the room, however tirelessly
you try, you can't quite reach the corner, even with your bristles

fully extended, because who is ever the right shape for that?
Or how the earth's weather—still astonishingly

unpredictable to humans—makes large swells
that lift and tip the ship just as you're mixing a cocktail.

And okay, it's not every day a cruise ship keels,
but can't you imagine the maddening spill?

You have one job and you can't do it right
when your world rolls too many degrees.

Sometimes there's no distinguishing the weeds
from the crops and you pull the wrong green.

Sometimes a bomb explodes at your touch
no matter your freedom from fear.

We all want to do our work well, harming no one.
We all recoil from the inefficient, the unforeseen,

the wasted and destroyed. None of us asked to be put here
holding something fragile in our hands. None of us knew

the ordinariness of our lives—the tasks and little
pleasures—counted up, would amount to so much ruin.

For such a time as this
Blair Benjamin

Esther 4:14

As we fear the possibilities this
battle year to come, I gift you small arms:
A tall blue *Fuck* mug for your evening tea;
Coetzee's *Waiting for the Barbarians*
for our bedside; *My Filter Needs To Be
Replaced* novelty socks; and a *This Is
My Protest Dishtowel* dishtowel.
There is no shame in repeating ourselves.

No one is above the law, we say again.
No one is above the law, we still believe.
Looks like this is your life now is the shit-
storm sign of our life now. So this is my
protest novelty sonnet—made to fit
your heart. And fuck subtle endings, my love.

Blair Benjamin's poetry has appeared or is forthcoming in *The Threepenny Review, Lumina, Spillway,* and *Typehouse*. He is the Director of the Studios at MASS MoCA residency program for artists and writers in North Adams, Massachusetts.

Big Guy
Jan Ball

The creepy big guy who shouts
for ketchup in a loud, demanding
voice at dinner at the nursing
home comes into the common
room and sits at the other end
of the long table that we are
sharing with my twin sister
who temporarily resides there
for post rehab.

We ask him if he'd like a brownie
and he says *yes* in a distorted voice
that seems to be coming from
another room and continues: *I have
brain damage,* elongating his vowels
as if he were thinking deeply.

He reaches over, closing the word
puzzle book that my husband observes
is very complicated, puts down
the brownie plate and extends
a meaty hand to me for a fist bump.

The skin on his knuckles is as soft
as a baby's.

[This poem was first published in *Founder's Favourites* (March 2020)]

Jan Ball started seriously writing poetry and submitting it for publication in 1998. Since then, she has had 309 poems accepted or published in the U.S., Australia, Canada, India, Ireland, Czech Republic and England. Published poems have appeared in: *ABZ, Atlanta Review, Calyx, Chiron, Main Street Rag, Phoebe* and many other journals. Her two chapbooks, *Accompanying Spouse* (2011) and *Chapter of Faults* (2014), have both been published by Finishing Line Press as well as Jan's first full length poetry collection, *I Wanted To Dance With My Father* (2017). Jan is a member of The Poetry Club of Chicago. She lived in Australia for fifteen years with her Australian husband, Ray Ball. Her two children, Geoffrey and Quentin, were born in Brisbane. Jan now lives in Chicago.

Window

Patrick Kalahar

I push my fingers against the pane of glass
Solid and cold, yet flexible
Disturbingly so
Because it's small deflection
Gives the illusion of mutability
As if it could be penetrated with a thought
But the window is a wall
The absolute limit
Of my world of this moment
It bars me from all intrusions
And it prevents me from leaping
To destruction on a sudden whim

This night the window is dark
Like a mirror of polished stone
Reflecting my rigid mouth and staring eyes
I could open the window, of course
But that would require a deliberate act
A decision
To let the bigger world in
Or let myself out
For now I am suspended
Like an incomplete thought
Between two possibilities
And the window remains a wall

Patrick Kalahar is a used & rare bookseller in Elwood, Indiana with his wife, poet and novelist Jenny. He is a book restorer, collector, and avid reader. His poems have appeared in anthologies published by Poets Unite Worldwide.

This Kitchen is a Mess
Hadley Austin

When I was 20, living
in a spider-infested room with
a shutter for a door, happy
simply to have anything door-like
because my room in the house before
had no door, my childhood friend came to visit
and she said of her future, "I expect to be wealthy,
but I don't expect to be particularly happy."

In that moment I expected to be happy, but I didn't expect to be particularly wealthy.

I remember in a moment of uncontrollable
high school anxiety wishing I could have the
contained, slim, placidity of Jackie Onassis.
When I was a child, we had on our refrigerator a cut out
image of Linda Hamilton from Terminator,
steel-jawed, and wielding a rifle that dwarfed her.

My childhood friend and I threw
our shoulders to the wheels
we weren't driving but
thought we were, and applied ourselves
to inner-city schools, to deep South
poverty pockets, to being Good Daughters,
to supporting our boyfriends, to getting degreed.

"But does it make you happy," my therapist would ask.
I was 31. "What is happiness?" I would reply.
Every week we would exchange these words.
There is power and comfort in ritual.

Happiness seemed absolutely abstract. A
conceited pursuit akin to catching a cloud.

I wanted a tattoo of Mary,
a woman powerful enough to answer prayers.
I had studied Kali in the shutter-door room,
her mouth dripping blood, wearing a necklace of skulls
rather than pearls, standing atop the monster
she'd been created to slay.
I wanted a tattoo of Mary,
and covered my apartment
with her image. A fifties vase from Florida,
porcelain white with her hands in prayer.

A hundred-year-old painting from Peru,
she stands serenely atop her crescent moon.
A candle, she is surrounded by roses.
I wanted a tattoo of Mary,
but couldn't bear to call her Virgin Mary,
just another woman whose value
was determined by what she did and did
not offer sexually.
I didn't want a tattoo of her with lilies,
and their associations with purity
and self-sacrifice, or with wheat
or pomegranates, as they were stand-ins
for fertility and I had to believe women have
power beyond that particular potency.

I did not get a tattoo of Mary.

I became obsessed with resurrection.

I am not Christian, nor have I ever been.

But resurrection abounds. With every
repair that allows my car to start again.
With every volunteer sunflower that
grows under the birdfeeder.
With every winter that becomes spring.

Resurrection has its limits. Of course.

I used to light candles for the dead at the altars
of empty churches, but now there are too many and
the candles all cost a dollar. They used
to cost a quarter.

I never lost the small-town habit
of scanning a sidewalk or a room for
people I know. I live in a big city now, and
am often far flung in travel. I often
see someone come back from the dead,
a grinning man in a trucker hat, or
a slim woman in pants three sizes too large
and then realize, no. They'd be older now.
That's what they looked like when we
were younger. They didn't even look
like that in the last years of their lives.
Why doesn't the brain delete
these people from the list of the possible?

I never see the walking ghosts of
those who died in old age, whose
minds had slipped and whose hands had
become frail. My subconscious doesn't
attempt correction for their absence.

"How did Jim die?" I asked his Texas drinking buddy at the wake.

"He shot himself in the face."

Ever since she said that sometimes when I close my eyes I see him sitting in a wooden
chair, a rifle between his knees, his face a destroyed bloody maw.

I craved cold places, went to
Iceland, read obsessively about the
Faroe Islands, Shetland Islands,
the Hebrides, the Aleutians.
In Whitehorse, Yukon Territory in
February I learned the temperature at
which eyelashes frost, metal burns the skin,
and fingernails freeze and peel.
I knit sweaters and watched crime shows set in
the Arctic. I learned to dogsled.

I discovered that when I'm anxious
and sad I clean the kitchen. I spent three
straight years without a dirty dish in
the sink. I have learned to mourn
efficiently. I am an expert mourner.

It came slowly. So slowly.

I moved to an apartment with a sunny
porch. I bought a hammock. All I wanted was
to sway, to rest one thousand rests
warmed by the sun. I would come home
from work in the middle of the day just to lay there.
 I'd collapse into the hammock before unlocking
the door, the cat sitting inside looking out at me with admonishment
from the window. When first we met, we spent an evening in
the hammock drinking tequila and reading poetry aloud. I poured
out of the hammock in a puddle of laughter at the night's end.

Two days after I began this poem, I got a call
from a friend whose voice now sounds
middle aged. "Chris is dead,"
he said. "I saw on Facebook."

Chris is, indeed, dead. Hang gliding
accident, he crashed into the Pacific and
drowned at a place called Devil's Slide,
according to Internet news stories.

People only remember Icarus flew too high,
but Daedalus also told him not to fly too low,
lest his wings be dampened by the sea, which would then
take him. The whole point was to escape Crete and live
to tell the tale, not make the adventure more adventurous.

But what, I suppose, is the fun in that?

They say drowning is a euphoric experience.

I saw pictures of his body in a small wooden box
smaller than a shoe box.
So strange that a body divorced
from its structures and fluids could
then occupy a space so small.

His ashes were returned to
the water where he drowned.

I close my eyes and see the ashes sitting on the surface of the water. Eddying. Their
slight weight bringing them ever so slowly down to the sea floor. I wish there had
been a way to suspend them in air forever.

This spring is unseasonably cool. I'm
in a sweater and I want it to be warm enough to
lay in the hammock with you. I am not afraid
of dying, but I am afraid
of loss and how little might remain if
our happiness collapsed, like a cake made
just as the rain comes in, and
the kitchen was clean again.

Hadley Austin is a Chicago based writer and filmmaker making a documentary about the legacy of uranium mining on the Navajo Nation.

Man to Man with the Folks' New Condo
D. R. James

I'm glad we have this chance to chat, now,
before my parents move in
for the rest of their lives.
There are things you need to know.

Frankly, they may not be easy
to get along with. Toast, for example,
the making of it, you see, for some reason
very important—how brown, how hot,
just when.
Essential things like that.

Remembering past trips, too,
can be irritating,
the details—which hotel,
in Warsaw, for God's sake,
where they first heard my sister
would divorce her first husband,
and just where that great Dutch
cheese place was, there,
in the mauve photo album,
a few pages after me in a tux,
the wedding.

They will tell you how they miss
all those rooms
in the house where they lived
for forty years this Wednesday,
coincidentally, my mother's
eighty-first birthday.

And whenever your 'foreign' gardeners
mow and trim the prim edges
of this emerald lawn
my parents will tell you how they dream
about their yard—all that grass,
the matured maples, the hedge of lilacs
defining the lot line out back.

You also need to know that you
were not their first choice.
They wanted the model
with the sunroom like their porch, to be
closer to the clubhouse, the workshop.
But they were told that could take
another couple of years,
maybe three or four or more,
and, as Mom puts it,
at this point they can't gamble,
what with Dad likely going
totally blind at any time,
and her just not able
to be their eyes and legs, both,
here, in a whole new place.

D. R. James has taught college writing, literature, and peace-making for 36 years and lives in the woods near Saugatuck, Michigan. His most recent of nine collections are *Flip Requiem* (Dos Madres Press, 2020), *Surreal Expulsion* (The Poetry Box, 2019), and *If god were gentle* (Dos Madres Press, 2017), and his micro-chapbook *All Her Jazz* is free, fun, and printable-for-folding at the Origami Poems Project. https://www.amazon.com/author/drjamesauthorpage

The Blessings of Spring
Philip C. Kolin

Summoned out of a dark chill
a season of light comes
to redeem stubble as pelting shadows
drift into the purple penance of dusk.

The air becomes chrism-scented
by soft breezes recovering
from winter coughs.

In a bounty of green,
trees rustle to touch each other
as if limbs and leaves were looking
for lost lovers.

In May's cotillion
bushes blush like girls in gala gowns
readying themselves for visits
from flirtatious beaux bees.

Even grubs and voles emerge
from shadowy clay clods
aburst with glowing.

Like traveling preachers
mallards in blue and green vestments
baptize ponds, creeks, rivers
rippling with their blessings.

In this season of radiance
the countryside looks like Eden
before the fall.

Philip C. Kolin, the Distinguished Professor of English (Emeritus) at the University of Southern Mississippi and the Editor Emeritus of the *Southern Quarterly*, has published nine collections of poems, the most recent being *Reaching Forever* (Poems for the Poiema Poetry Series of Cascade Press, 2019). Kolin has also published extensively on Shakespeare and Tennessee Williams.

Healing Nature
Lylanne Musselman

I hear songbirds chirping and feel calm,
a respite from a world that's filled
with, guns, gaudy lies, and fake news.
A world where my mom talks
to my dead grandma as if she's in
the backseat of my car,
asking what she wants to order
from Dairy Queen. Where mom's falls
become more frequent, where I feel
like her mother telling her to go
to the bathroom, when to go to bed,
that she needs to eat. She fights me
about her bedtime as if she's ten,
I fight with myself as to how much longer
I can deal with being her caregiver,
as she looks at me and asks where I went,
why I won't tell her where her mom is.
The outside world is fighting too
over how much more we can take
without someone to protect us
from the violence, the lies, the poverty.
It's hard not to give up. But the birds
ground me with their frequency – their songs
lift me to Zen, a state where I long to live.

Lylanne Musselman is a native Hoosier and resides in Indianapolis, Indiana. She teaches creative writing classes at Ivy Tech Community College in Indianapolis, and at the University of Indianapolis' School of Adult Learning. Lylanne is a regular contributor on WFHB radio's BloomingOUT with her story feature L WordS. An award winning poet, her poetry has appeared or is forthcoming in *Flying Island, New Voices News, Etchings, Tipton Poetry Journal, Poetry Motel*, and many TallGrass Writers Guild Anthologies.

Basic Facts about the Paper My Husband has been Staring at for Weeks
Timothy Robbins

It was pulled from a legal pad. The
sheet's bottom is curled and worn to
a texture resembling flannel. It exudes

an air of devotion to him which fits
his air of devotion to it. He is more
restless than it. He scratches his nape

and twists in his seat and shrugs one
shoulder when thoughts stirred by
the fan ruffle his hair as wind stirs

watching. The paper shows patience
that matches its devotion. If you
saw it you'd probably think it was

a Russian Constuctivist painting (not
math), a license or a mandala for a one-
celled guru's biological meditation.

Timothy Robbins has been teaching English as a Second Language for 28 years. His poems have appeared in *Main Street Rag, Off The Coast, Bayou Magazine, Slant, Tipton Poetry Journal, Cholla Needles* and many others. He has published three volumes of poetry: *Three New Poets* (Hanging Loose Press), *Denny's Arbor Vitae* (Adelaide Books) and *Carrying Bodies* (Main Street Rag Press). He lives in Wisconsin with his husband of 22 years.

Text from the exotic pets aisle
Timothy Pilgrim

Fire ants gather, bury their dead,
keep service short, return to work.
They crawl glassed-in lives, carry

a thousand times their weight,
dig through passage sand, wend,
climb, turn. Two may touch,

tap out a brief embrace, make ways past,
take separate tunnels,
freshly dug, hopeless prisoners,

no escape. Forgive me, sweet, I wander on.
Texting to say, four stops remain —
a couple Petcos, two stores at the mall.

Keep candles lit, your red wine, warm.
I'll slip in the back way,
we'll make love in the hall.

Timothy Pilgrim, Bellingham, Washington, a Pacific Northwest poet and 2018 Pushcart Prize nominee with several hundred acceptances by journals such as *Seattle Review, Cirque, San Pedro River Review, Toasted Cheese, Windsor Review, Hobart, Sleet Magazine* and *Third Wednesday,* is author of *Mapping water* (Flying Trout Press, 2016). See www.timothypilgrim.org for all his poetry.

Narcolepsy
Ron Riekki

My girlfriend has cataplexy
if she experiences too much emotion—
especially sadness or laughing.

On the day before Thanksgiving, Trump
posts a photo of himself as a shirtless boxer.
I turn my computer to her and say,
"Check this out" and suddenly
she falls to the floor, unable to move.
She's like this for about a half minute,
like Trump had knocked her out.

She blinks her eyes, coming back to the room.
"Hilarious," I say.
"No," she says, "Just sad."

Ron Riekki's books include *U.P.* (Ghost Road Press), *Posttraumatic* (Hoot 'n' Waddle), and *My Ancestors are Reindeer Herders and I Am Melting in Extinction* (Loyola University Maryland's Apprentice House Press). Riekki co-edited *Undocumented* (Michigan State University Press) and *The Many Lives of The Evil Dead* (McFarland), and edited *And Here* (MSU Press), *Here* (MSU Press, Independent Publisher Book Award), and *The Way North* (Wayne State University Press, Michigan Notable Book).

The Day After I Came Back
William Pruitt

John came to my door at 11 p.m. Sunday night.
This was the day after I came back from New York
where I spent time with old friends and had a day
to wonder if we were the same people we were then.

John needed a ride to the bus stop,
where his sister and her four year-old awaited him.
He was going back to Greenville Technical College
in the morning. He and sister were tending
to their mother one block over who just
had a triple bypass. She had moved here
from South Carolina for health care. They were preparing
to sue her doctor-- I guess the one they moved away from--
as soon as they could hire a lawyer. John's other sister's
father-in-law was chief of police in a nearby town.
Later he would be forced to resign when charged
with rubber stamping background checks
for an officer who pressured a prisoner for sex
and for covering for a cop on cocaine who
hit a pregnant woman with his car and drove away.
The chief would say it was the town supervisor
who wanted the abuser hired without questions, the same
sup who was found to have not murdered the woman
he had secretly been having sex with,
who had been stabbed by her unstable
adult son. But this all happened after
I took John to the bus stop, to wait with Amanda
and her four year-old son
who had just lost a tooth.

William Pruitt is a writer, storyteller and assistant editor for *Narrative Magazine*. He has published poems in such places as *Ploughshares, Anderbo.com, Cottonwood, Country Journal, Ravensperch, Otis Nebula* and *Stoneboat*; in two chapbooks from White Pine and FootHills; and the self-published *Walking Home* from the Eastman House. His short stories appear in recent issues of *Indiana Voice Journal, Adelaide Literary Review, Oyster River Pages, Sick Lit, Crack the Spine Literary Magazine, Visitant, Midway* and *Hypertext*, and in an upcoming issue of *The Woven Tale Press*. William lives in Rochester, New York.

Dear Time
Vivian Wagner

You seem to be speeding
up lately, a tugboat gaining
traction in a muddy river.
You've always been good
at understanding geography,
the way movement happens
between water and stone,
and so I defer to you, trust
that you know everything
and regret nothing.
Still, though, could I have
a minute, or a space between
minutes, just to be?
I'll catch up; I promise.
I just need to stop and breathe,
rest while the sun seems
almost still, and herons flap
large wings overhead, aiming
for the next branch's repose.

Vivian Wagner is an associate professor of English at Muskingum University in New Concord, Ohio. Her essays and poems have appeared in *Slice Magazine, Muse/A Journal, Forage Poetry Journal, Pittsburgh Poetry Review, McSweeney's Internet Tendency, Gone Lawn, The Atlantic, Narratively, The Ilanot Review, Silk Road Review, Zone 3*, and other publications. She's the author of a memoir, *Fiddle: One Woman, Four Strings, and 8,000 Miles of Music* (Citadel-Kensington); a full-length poetry collection, *Raising* (Clare Songbirds Publishing House); and three poetry chapbooks: *The Village* (Aldrich Press-Kelsay Books), *Making* (Origami Poems Project), and *Curiosities* (Unsolicited Press).

Permanence

Bruce Levine

The presence of the day
Holding forth like a Beethoven symphony
Yielding its power to the aftermath of flight
Soaring on wings of golden glory
Vespers held in a Cathedral
While transfixed
Transformed into a dream
Suspended in time and repeated
As the presence of a new day
Enlightens the soul
Giving way to the transience of minutes
Fading at once then reunited into hours
With the permanence of forever

Bruce Levine, a 2019 Pushcart Prize Poetry Nominee, has spent his life as a writer of fiction and poetry and as a music and theatre professional. Over 300 of his works are published in over 25 on-line journals including *Ariel Chart, Friday Flash Fiction, Literary Yard;* over 30 print books including *Poetry Quarterly, Haiku Journal, Dual Coast Magazine*, and his shows have been produced in New York and around the country. Six eBooks are available from Amazon.com. His work is dedicated to the loving memory of his late wife, Lydia Franklin. He lives in New York with his dog, Daisy. Visit him at www.brucelevine.com.

The Crosswalk
James Mulhern

Today I saw a father and son
stepping onto the crosswalk.
I braked and watched them pass.
Son on father's shoulders,
headed to the park with swings.

I drove on, thinking of you
and wondered why you
never lifted me and held my legs
or brought me to the swings.
But you were not that type of father.

Once, we built a shed together.
I heard you say at a family party years later,
"Remember when Danny and I built the shed."
But it wasn't my brother
who cut wood and hammered nails with you.

I was bothered just a bit.
I had other memories,
like when you held my hands as we knotted my tie,
how we both looked in the mirror,
and I saw myself in your face.

You patted my shoulders.
Someone crossed the room and paused to take a picture.
It was on the table by your coffin. Your hands on mine.
Proof that we had closeness for a moment,
and that is enough.

James Mulhern lives in Florida and has published over seventy times in literary journals and anthologies. In 2015, Mr. Mulhern was awarded a fully paid writing fellowship to Oxford University in the United Kingdom. That same year, a story was longlisted for the Fish Short Story Prize. In 2017, he was nominated for a Pushcart Prize. His most recent novel, *Give Them Unquiet Dreams*, is a Readers' Favorite Book Award winner, a Notable Best Indie Book of 2019, and a Kirkus Reviews Best Book of 2019.

electric lemon
Michael Chang

You know the story
He became the rain
Then a roaring fire
Face impassive
Flames licking warm & thick & ferocious
The furl of his shirt in hot air
The room glowed
The walls cracked & fissured
The ceiling deposited poisonous fruit
It was a forest & then it wasn't
She watched the boy disappear into a man
& the man disappear into a desert
When the basement started filling with foxes
They vowed never to play house again

Michael Chang (they/them) is the proud recipient of a Brooklyn Poets fellowship. They were invited to attend the *Kenyon Review* Writers Workshop at Kenyon College as well as the Omnidawn Poetry Writing Conference at Saint Mary's College of California. Their writing has been published or is forthcoming in *The Minnesota Review, Yellow Medicine Review, Heavy Feather Review, UCityReview, Love's Executive Order, Glass Mountain, Thin Air, ellipsis... literature & art, Q/A Poetry, Yes Poetry, Typo Mag, Wrath-Bearing Tree, Bending Genres, The Hunger, Cabildo Quarterly, Willawaw Journal, Neon Garden, The Conglomerate, Queen Mob's Tea House, Funny Looking Dog Quarterly, London Grip, Rogue Agent, Kissing Dynamite, BULL Fiction, Literary Orphans, Animal: A Beast of a Literary Magazine, Collective Unrest, Pink Plastic House, Little Rose, Milk + Beans, Squawk Back*, and many others. Michael lives in New Jersey.

Hypercatelectic at the Indiana Historical Society Museum
Michael Brockley

> Hypercatelectic: having an extra syllable or syllables at the end of a metrically complete verse or in a metrical foot

Shelley and I sit in the Cole Porter Room, a mock cabaret with no wine menu nor barkeep. On the dais a young woman sings the Hoosier's greatest hits lists. "Anything Goes." "I Love Paris." "Ain't Misbehavin'." She lifts her thin voice into a microphone that looks like a miniature gladiator helmet. Behind her the songwriter's ghost tickles a glissando from the piano. When the chanteuse De-loveleys *You've won my heart and I've lost my brain*, Shelley and I chuckle. And raise our hands as if to order another round of merlot. After leaving the Porter tribute room, we wander through the gallery's exhibits, wondering at the shotgun shacks of Richmond, the legacy of railroad men, and the eccentricities of Methodist circuit rider Lorenzo Dow. Over coffee in the basement cafe, I misquote the lost brain line from "De-lovely," singing I have a dangerous brain in a world of saxophone players, forever wars, and Republicans who scheme to steal elections. Shelley asks if I've ever heard the voices that speak from the borders where dreams and memories blur, having correctly remembered the lost brain phrasing. Asks if I always misquote the wrong words. I smile at her across our caffeinated drinks. Her espresso. My toffee nut latte with almond milk. Beneath the vault of Hoosier history, we plot our misbehavior.

Slow Turning

A Cento for John Hiatt

Michael Brockley

I head south. And try not to think about her while I drive. Love gets strange. In the end, we taught each other how to make a broken heart. All dust down a country road tonight. I've crossed so many muddy waters that love isn't where I thought I left it. A perfectly good guitar on the back seat floor keeps the melody for the old voices on the radio that map my runaway. I'm traveling one of those roads where it always feels like rain. From my edge of the razor old habits are hard to break. What wouldn't I give for a sign. A light. One lipstick sunset. Just knowing that the rivers know my name. I promise no more wicked grins. I might already be a winner, stealing moments from the time I loved a hurricane. Have a little faith in me.

Michael Brockley is a retired school psychologist who lives in Muncie, Indiana. His poems have appeared in *Atticus Review, Third Wednesday,* and *Jokes Review*. Poems are forthcoming in *Hobo Camp Review, Live Nude Poems,* and *Indianapolis Anthology*.

Albino
Mary Hills Kuck

In the balcony above the solarium we sat, legs crossed,
our urban-weary eyes lapping moonlight spilling
into the wooded yard. Fireflies punctuated velvet air.
Crickets sawed, tree frogs bayed across the spread.

Some low-lying leaves shivered, and a ghostly figure
moved along the line of trees. We followed it,
eyes wide, to the edge of swamp. *Perhaps,* you said,
a big white cat, but likely not a crouching man.

It rustled into brush and we leaned together,
marvelling that we were here to share this
woodland with the wildlife and the grass.
The moon arced; darkness wrapped us.

Later in the week I rose early, stepped lightly
to the rim of the ravine, rising sun behind me
rouging trees and sky. I wanted to give thanks
for all the green, the swampy pond, the wild.

As I breathed the life of woods, I sensed
a being at my side and looked down into grass.
A pearly face with pudgy cheeks and feather tail
locked me with her pink-tinged eyes.

Her body white, her whiskers milky mild, the beast
bewitched me with her grace. At last I saw the danger
that the alabaster skunk-like shape conferred.
We both stood absolutely still, silently evaluating risk.

I waited for the dreaded turn of tail, but, what a gift,
she trusted me and slipped back down the cliff.

Having retired from teaching English and Communications, first in the US and for many years in Jamaica, **Mary Hills Kuck** now lives with her family in Massachusetts. She has received a Pushcart Prize Nomination and her poems have appeared in *Long River Run, Connecticut River Review, Hamden Chronicle, SIMUL: Lutheran Voices in Poetry, Caduceus, The Jamaica Observer, Fire Stick: A Collection of New & Established Caribbean Poets, Massachusetts State Poetry Society, Inc. Anthology , the Aurorean, Tipton Poetry Journal,* and others.

Ivan

Douglas Cole

There's a man I call Ivan going through rapid opening cartoon doors
awakening mid-March with an anniversary in the back of his mind
he's momentarily forgetting as he slides by pampas grass in waist-high
vases the woman brought from Padilla Bay now with little silvery feelers
floating off and clinging to the outline he just left as he plows through
mountains of air shaped like The Brothers and he's sort of a brother of mine
slogging through court cases and church services and branch meetings
late morning subway rides and burials and bewildering resurrections
closing a book on a finger and looking up as if he just heard something
as I go on alone with that outline still there in the air behind me

Boethius Said

Douglas Cole

The butcher spends his life in blood and guts, the professor in his books.
When their cities flood, fire ants band together and make a floating island
from the bodies of the dead. I am stepping from the mountain top
into chest-sinking freedom. I know some of you are saying, really?
in disbelief. Should be snuffed out for good! as I slide on shoes of light
and stroll through the blazing kingdom with hands behind my back.

Douglas Cole has published six collections of poetry and a novella. His work has appeared in several anthologies as well as *The Chicago Quarterly Review, The Galway Review, Bitter Oleander, Louisiana Literature* and *Slipstream*. He has been nominated twice for a Pushcart and Best of the Net and received the Leslie Hunt Memorial Prize in Poetry. He lives and teaches in Seattle. His website is douglastcole.com.

Yahweh Sabaoth
Patrick Theron Erickson

Ezekiel 37:1-14

Dead men's bones

you can't stir them
with a stick

But let a choice word
be said

well-spoken

and there is
a rattling

as bone
comes together
with bone

Sinews appear
and ligaments and tendons
abound

Flesh covers them
and breath enters them

and they stand
upon their feet
one vast army

and at their head

erect
fleet of foot
battle-ready

Yahweh Sabaoth.

Patrick Theron Erickson, a resident of Garland, Texas is a retired parish pastor put out to pasture himself. His work has appeared in *Tipton Poetry Journal, Grey Sparrow Journal,* and *The Main Street Rag*, among other publications, and more recently in *Torrid Literature Journal, South Florida Poetry Journal, Arlington Literary Journal and Sheila-Na-Gig*.

Nestbuilding in a Difficult Season
Doris Lynch

After a line from Mary Oliver's poem: "Swimming, One Day in August"

Among the flux of happenings,
this, a pandemic. As the robin ferries
twig after twig onto a fork of the old magnolia,
an American dies every forty-seven seconds.
With her beak, the bird tests each wind-tossed
limblet, then begins lifting, ferrying and
engineering it into the exact right spot.
On the deck this spring-infused morning, we stand
as a covey of redbuds brighten the grey sky,
the last daffodils waft in April breezes, and hundreds
of falling magnolia blossoms paint a wide
spiral of white and pink on the back lawn.

Doris Lynch lives in Bloomington, Indiana and has recent work in *Flying Island, Frogpond, Modern Haiku, Contemporary Haibun Online, Drifting Sands Haibun* and in the anthologies: *Cowboys & Cocktails: Poetry from the True Grit Saloon*, Brick Street Poetry Inc., 2019, *Red River book of Haibun*, Red River Press, New Delhi, Indiana, 2019, and *Another Trip Around the Sun: 365 Days of Haiku for Children Young and Old*, Brooks Books, 2019.

Isaac Aloft
James Green

The eyes say it all,

they say it through the unfocused lens of the camera,
through pupils rinsed and dried in the darkroom,
they say to the father, unmistakably the father, slinging

the boy into the clouds, hands to hands, round and round
spinning the boy, feet scribing an arc across the sky:
I am safe in your grasp, faster! higher! high as the sun!

Like Abraham, feet planted firmly on the ground,
the father lifts the boy toward heaven.
Like Issac aloft, the boy rises in the grasp of the father,

although this Isaac exhilarates the expanse with shrieks
of laughter, rises as one with the father into the clouds
into the grainy sands of the photographed sky,

eyes shouting faster! higher! innocent of peril.
Attached at the wrists, the father points his son's toes
to a heaven of hearts and the God of Abraham.

Abraham meant to give up his son. Not this father.
A wrinkle in the photograph makes a crease across
the time it takes to hold on or let go.

The eyes say it all.

James Green has worked as a naval officer, deputy sheriff, high school English teacher, professor of education, and administrator in both public schools and universities. Recipient of two Fulbright grants, he has served as a visiting scholar at the University of Limerick in Ireland and the National Chung Cheng University in Taiwan. In addition to academic publications, including three books, Green is the author of three chapbooks of poetry and a fourth, *Long Journey Home*, is forthcoming after winning the Charles Dickson Chapbook Contest sponsored by the Georgia Poetry Society., Individual poems have appeared in literary magazines in England, Ireland, and the United States. He resides in Muncie, Indiana.

Inward

Daniel Edward Moore

is the one direction people despise the most,
                shunned like an Amish addict in the barn

planting a Turkish flower in his arm
                to make his escape from a wireless world

who's never heard his name on twitter
                never seen his Facebook page

wet with men dripping pitchforks & hay
                praising the creator of distance at dawn

just minutes before udders are squeezed
                & mouths are filled with a pint of perfection

white as the powder that sings his name
                from the glorious throat of a spoon.

Daniel Edward Moore lives in Washington on Whidbey Island. He has poems forthcoming in Weber Review, The Cape Rock, Kestrel, The Phoenix, Red Earth Review, RipRap, The Timberline Review, Capsule Stories, River Heron Review, Passages North, and Eastern Iowa Review. He is the author of two chapbooks, *Confessions of a Pentecostal Buddhist* (CreateSpace) and *Boys* (Duck Lake Books). *Waxing the Dents*, a full length collection, is from Brick Road Poetry Press. Visit him at Danieledwardmoore.com.

The Contour of the Line
Barry Peters

1

The alarm cleans
the chaos of the dream,
throws in motion

your grand plan
to set things in order
before the day gets away,

yolks dropping
out of their shells,
the other eggs

warmly blanketed
so you can carry them
to market and sell,

tongue untwisted,
balance sheet balanced,
everything in working order.

2

The whiffle ball,
bumbling like a bee
in backyard wind,

fluttering hither and thither,
yon and yon and yon.
It's summer,

the clock's hands
in its pockets
jiggling change,

waiting. Soon enough
a big kid uncorks
a fastball at your face

that magically curves
over home plate.
You whiff again.

3

The trumpeter
crosses his arms,
cradles the shimmering

brass over his heart.
He understands
your anxiety.

He leans over,
whiskey breath
whispering the secret:

The charts are so fast,
it's impossible to hit
all the notes all the time.

Sometimes it's good
enough just to play
the contour of the line.

Barry Peters lives in Durham and teaches in Raleigh, North Carolina. Publications *include The American Journal of Poetry, Best New Poets 2018, New Ohio Review, Poetry East* and *Rattle*.

Tree's Bones

Richard Dinges, Jr.

Cottonwood's dead bones
still reach into
a blank sky. Each
year, twigs break off,
branches shatter,
fewer birds gather
in black cyphers.
Bleached bones fall,
a scatter around
cottonwood's solid
trunk, too thick for
me to gather
into my arms
after I trip
through its bone field,
look up into
its soaring spire,
knowing I will
never reach so high.

Richard Dinges, Jr. lives in Nebraska, has an MA in literary studies from University of Iowa, and no longer manages information systems at an insurance company. *Green Hills Literary Lantern, Westview, Pinyon, Writers Bloc,* and *Big Windows Review* most recently accepted his poems for their publications.

Mars

Casey Killingsworth

There was this show on the massive amount of food
prepared everyday on a luxury ship, thousands
of pounds of shrimp and chicken and unspeakable
numbers of workers trapped on that boat,
racing against the clock to make every meal perfect.
I don't even know if we have words to judge this.
Sometimes I don't feel like I belong here, like I'm
different in the way a shrimp is different
from a chicken, the way they look at
the world with either feathers or from
underneath the ocean and in the end sharing
space on someone's plate is all they have in common.
Sometimes I feel like I'm from another planet,
you know, like I'm lying there on someone else's plate.
Then I walk down the street watching everyone watch
themselves in store windows believing the same thing,
how different they are. And I start thinking, well, maybe
we are all from Mars or maybe we're already on Mars
and we've been here all along.
And if that's true, then maybe we're not so different after all.

Casey Killingsworth has work in *The American Journal of Poetry, Kimera, Spindrift, Rain, Slightly West, Timberline Review, COG, Common Ground Review, Typehouse, Bangalore Review, Two Thirds North*, and other journals. His book of poems, *A Handbook for Water*, was published by Cranberry Press in 1995. As well he has a book on the poetry of Langston Hughes, *The Black and Blue Collar Blues* (VDM, 2008). Casey lives in Washington and has a Master's degree from Reed College.

Fort Lauderdale
J.P. Check

Art Credit: J.P. Check

We call her Ariel for hair
Red herring red. She sleeps under
The pier. Her friends are girls the same as her,

Discarded by hardnosed mothers
And egghead fathers.
You didn't hate her perfect, junonia

Shell skin. It hadn't gotten her
past the pier,
After all.

You can't see the hunger waxing in her belly
When she dances behind an industrial house beat.
She's been at all the clubs on the strip.

I asked her why she came out tonight,
"I want to be where the people are."
She says, "I want to see 'em dancing."

J.P. Check is a writer and illustrator from rural North Alabama. His poetry and paintings are influenced by his hometown and the South at large.

Battleship

Duane Anderson

She said she was playing battleship,
a game of hits and misses,
and it was all hits for her today,
not sinking any battleships

with all of her hits,
but sticking the needle in the vein
and each time drawing blood on the
first try. A perfect record,

nothing less but what was expected
to each laying down on the beds
as they donated a unit of their blood.
It was smooth sailing in calm waters.

Duane Anderson currently lives in La Vista, Nebraska, and volunteers with a non-profit organization as a Donor Ambassador on their blood drives. He has had poems published in *The Pangolin Review, Fine Lines, The Sea Letter, Cholla Needles, Tipton Poetry Journal, Adelaide Literary Magazine* and several other publications.

Regarding Rilke
Wally Swist

for Art Beck

I just want to relay the richness I am grateful
for in our exchange regarding Rilke. That insight that
Rilke intended to portray that both Jesus

and Magdalen were *in love* with *the illusion* of Christ's
divinity is just stunning; and
that in the poem "The Garden of Olives," on the eve of

his death, Jesus becomes aware that the Lord
he imagines in his conversation through his prayer,
most likely doesn't exist, is breathtaking. Additionally,

the point that you revised the title of "Der Auferstandene"
from "The Resurrected" to "The Risen" to provide
the nuance, and the intended ambiguity, whether it is

Mary Magdalen who has *risen* rather than Christ,
who may only be *resurrected* through the transformation
of his disciples, and not physically, is thoroughly

mesmerizing and offers continued and active
amazement. And, as you point out, nowhere in Rilke's
later work, including *New Poems,* does he offer

love as a concept, and that these poems are specific
to *things*, after his work with and his influence by Rodin—
as you mention, his poems regarding

Orpheus, Eurydice, and Hermes aren't about love at all; although, of course, Rilke does portray Orpheus' relationship with Eurydice as being his failure to love.

Wally Swist's books include *Huang Po and the Dimensions of Love* (Southern Illinois University Press, 2012), selected by Yusef Komunyakaa as co-winner in the 2011 Crab Orchard Series Open Poetry Contest, and *A Bird Who Seems to Know Me: Poems Regarding Birds & Nature* (Ex Ophidia Press, 2019), the winner of the 2018 Ex Ophidia Press Poetry Prize. His recent poems have or will appear in *Commonweal, Rattle,* and *Transference: A Literary Journal Featuring the Art & Process of Translation*. Recent books include *The Bees of the Invisible* (2019) and *Evanescence: Selected Poems* (2020), both with Shanti Arts. He currently lives in Massachusetts.

Silver Fire
Nathaniel Dolton-Thornton

the grass held up its lamp
the night's wick was dry

after a summer like that
the grass was in withdrawal

it could feel a whole pack of patties
on its back that needed roasting

the grass had wanted the lighter
he said

the grass had asked for it

Nathaniel Dolton-Thornton's poems have appeared or are forthcoming in *Tin House, Prelude, Poetry Salzburg Review, Griffith Review, Sycamore Review, TAB, The Account, Raritan,* and other publications. He studies political ecology as a Marshall Scholar at the University of Cambridge.

Questions
William Snyder, Jr.

Students sit in neat, long rows. Professors clump
like Rushmores in the easiest chairs. Our poet
reads. Poems about death. Her husband's.
His dying after years together and her long days
after—the garden, the rain, the desire.
A widow now, she lives in a widow's house.

I think of my father—the thick, square jaw,
the rulered lips of his dissatisfaction. My mother—
her gray skin, the oxygen sucked like waning
nectar from a plastic tube. I have their lives
in fragments, in bits—Nashville in '45,
the collie dog in Hartford, all of us by Lake Lucerne—
little squares in a shoebox, dates in nib-penned
black on white, purfled borders.

Memories are random now, and fading, like
those photos, but I have questions still—they do not
fade. Why mother cried those nights
I lay awake—cancer, she'd say, it must be cancer,
and father saying, no, no, it isn't, it can't be,
but if you don't stop smoking. Or how we left
Plattsburg—brothers and I and father—
how we said goodbye to mother. Did she hold us?
And when he'd say, years after, *if I'd only known
what I know now—movies, TV—what
they show, you can learn so much,* and I'd
ask if it would've made a difference.

I imagine our poet still has questions too—though
she can ask them now in poems. And these students,
their questions, so many yet to ask. The profs?
Well, they know the answers already, before
they're even asked, like a bunch of Carnacs.

William Snyder, Jr. has published poems in *Atlanta Review*, *Poet Lore*, and *Southern Humanities Review* among others. He was the co-winner of the 2001 Grolier Poetry Prize; winner of the 2002 Kinloch Rivers Chapbook competition; The CONSEQUENCE Prize in Poetry, 2013; the 2015 Claire Keyes Poetry Prize; Tulip Tree Publishing Stories That Need To Be Told 2019 Merit Prize for Humor; and Encircle Publications 2019 Chapbook Contest. He lives in Fargo, North Dakota and teaches writing and literature at Concordia College in Moorhead, Minnesota.

Parting Ways
Danielle Wong

she watches him text privately in their room
silence sits cross-legged between them

he does not hear her voice, feel her fingers lightly reach for him
a cloak of darkness falls upon her

she desires her mate; he is with another
pain tears at her skin and slips underneath her nails

Grim Reaper smiles and carefully wraps her in his cloak

Danielle Wong lives in Quebec and is the author of *Bubble Fusion*, a collection of poems about raising a child with autism. Her other work has appeared in *Soft Cartel*, *Montreal Writes*, *Patterns*, and other anthologies. She enjoys losing herself in forests, but can be found at https://www.daniellewong.ca.

Photo credit: Ben Di Nunzio

The T-Shirt Says *Breaking News*
Gabriel Welsch

and then *I don't care*,
as if that is news,
as if it is anything other
than breaking.

Every pickup sold here
sports *extreme* decaled on a tailgate,
paid for with a re-enlistment bonus,
and *breaking news* drives one.

Breaking news wears the hat
to Make America Great Again.
She and I agree: every bit of news
is breaking something.

Another shirt says *no hate*
in a parade of bigots
marching on our streets for
Patriot's Day, breaking

my ability to avoid
a cliché so wounded and drained
where buildings are so more than empty
their shade darkens loss the more.

Ours is the only county in the state
without an interstate, with no
quick road to elsewhere, no break
in the trees, no break in the mountains

and no interest in making one.

Gabriel Welsch writes fiction and poetry and is the author of four collection of poems, the most recent of which is *The Four Horsepersons of a Disappointing Apocalypse* (Steel Toe Books, 2013). His work appears recently or will appear in *Ploughshares, Asheville Poetry Review, Atticus Review, Lake Effect, Bodega Magazine, Bluestem, Pembroke Review,* and *trampset*. He lives in Pittsburgh with his family, and works as vice president of marketing and communications at Duquesne University.

Painting lesson
Katie Richards

Prussian blue waves curve like vertebrae
then burst on cliff's edge. Cadmium
daffodils break through ragged rock.
Foliage brush pounds blossom into being.
Flowers blown sideways are bodies bent
in prayer. Sometimes we know in the back-
ground wave foam hides behind cliff's form
pressed hard against horizon. Fan brush
swirls day's sky to dusk. Progesterone
cream swirls cold on my belly, my thigh,
sits thick on my shin, until I rub it all in
twice daily. Circular motion again and
again on my skin. This painting,
the way I keep my pregnancies in.

Katie Richards is an MFA candidate at George Mason University. She is the recipient of the 2016 Mark Craver Poetry Award and the 2020 Mary Roberts Rinehart Poetry Award. Her poetry has previously appeared in the *South Dakota Review* and is forthcoming in the *North Dakota Quarterly*. She currently lives in the DC metro area with her husband and children.

A Bus Commute Home
J.J. Steinfeld

The late-afternoon commuter
fleeing an office that day after day
scrapes his soul, steals his time,
thinks a harsh mantra in rhythm
with the bus's grating movement:
the end of everything today
the end of everything tomorrow
the end of everything in a hundred years
the end of everything in a billion years…

then mesmerized by the relentless second hand
of an old watch on the wrist of the young woman
standing next to him on the crammed bus
her left hand holding the overhead metal bar
his right hand tired from gripping too tightly
his thoughts find another destination

first the word *love* comforts him
then the word *eternal*
eternal love, he thinks
gripping even tighter
the bus almost dissolves
a film of his life revised:
courtship, marriage, a life together

the old watch disappears
as the young woman leaves
the bus a stop before his:
the end of the everything today…

Canadian poet, fiction writer, and playwright **J. J. Steinfeld** lives on Prince Edward Island, where he is patiently waiting for Godot's arrival and a phone call from Kafka. While waiting, he has published 20 books, including *Identity Dreams and Memory Sounds* (Poetry, Ekstasis Editions, 2014), *Madhouses in Heaven, Castles in Hell* (Stories, Ekstasis Editions, 2015), *An Unauthorized Biography of Being* (Stories, Ekstasis Editions, 2016), *Absurdity, Woe Is Me, Glory Be* (Poetry, Guernica Editions, 2017), *A Visit to the Kafka Café* (Poetry, Ekstasis Editions, 2018), and *Gregor Samsa Was Never in The Beatles* (Stories, Ekstasis Editions, 2019). His short stories and poems have appeared in numerous periodicals and anthologies internationally, and over 50 of his one-act plays and a handful of full-length plays have been performed in Canada and the United States.

Impossible Passages #77
Glen Armstrong

Okay. So, sheet lightning, not the paranormal, ignites the bellies of purple clouds. Knowing does not make it less unnerving. I am driving home from the carnival. It starts to rain. There are no stars.

By all accounts, splendid times were had. The generators hummed, and sugar shared its incredible body with air. Everyone who wanted a fortune received one, the future printed clearly enough to read as unusual fire, crudely painted yellows and reds, continuously spun.

I am trying to remember the seven wonders of the ancient world. I am steeping tea and listening as two male voices bend reality on the radio. One of them would have us believe that a secret society of travelers visits us once a year from their city beyond the stars. The other would have us believe that there are no stars.

Glen Armstrong holds an MFA in English from the University of Massachusetts, Amherst and teaches writing at Oakland University in Rochester, Michigan. He edits a poetry journal called *Cruel Garters* and has two current books of poems: *Invisible Histories* and *The New Vaudeville*. His work has appeared in *Poetry Northwest*, *Conduit*, and *Cream City Review*.

Inscription Written in Water
Lois Marie Harrod

after Jorge Luis Borge's "Inscription"

For the great seas transmuting the atlas
and the great oceans trimming the world.
For the rivers that flow near me every day,
the Stony Brook and the Millstone moving towards the Delaware.
For the rivers beyond with their lovely names,
the Rappahonnock and the Chesapeake, Gila and Chilkat.
For the muddied Mississippi and the Sarno
with its strange green waters and the wasted Marilao
dividing Manila where a child's rubber slippers
are slipping downstream.
Or for the Rio Grande
where the child floats with her father.
For the Jordan which I was once taught
to revere, the Jordon
where John baptized a man
who had little idea his teachings would be used
to abuse small boys
and contaminate other streams.

Lois Marie Harrod's latest collection *Woman* was published by Blue Lyra in February 2020. Her *Nightmares of the Minor Poet* appeared in June 2016 from Five Oaks; her chapbook *And She Took the Heart* appeared in January 2016; *Fragments from the Biography of Nemesis* (Cherry Grove Press) and the chapbook *How Marlene Mae Longs for Truth* (Dancing Girl Press) appeared in 2013. A Dodge poet, she is published in literary journals and online ezines from *American Poetry Review* to *Zone 3*. She teaches at the Evergreen Forum in Princeton and at The College of New Jersey. Links to her online work www.loismarieharrod.org

3 A.M. in the CICU
Renee Emerson

The midnight nudge of the phone call:
everyday she is dying, and some days
more than others. What to do

with the other children? Drop
your bag of groceries to catch
the falling apple tossed to you
by God. (I set them down
by my legs.

Some judge me for that)
and it fell and bruised—
a dark applesauce in the sweet white.

What are you running away
from when you run
into this burning building?
Cradled fire like a Pentecost, learned
a language I refuse to speak.

Gifts are left in paper bags
on the sticky-wheeled food tray:
a handmade bow, a muslin blanket,
the onion-thin promises of scripture,

I held her, with tubes crocodile snapped
to my shirt, with her wires through my fingers.
I wrote down everything they said. I still do.

Renee Emerson was born in Tennessee and resides in Missouri. She has published poems in magazines such as *Perspectives, Still,* and *Valley Voices,* and currently teaches online courses for various universities. She is the author of *Keeping Me Still* (Winter Goose Publishing 2014) and *Threshing Floor* (Jacar Press 2016), and is online at www.ReneeEmerson.wordpress.com

Empty City
Marjie Giffin

The people have all gone inside;
the sounds of the city have died
and a soft silence like snow has fallen
all over the street lamps and crossings
and benches where talking has ceased.

The co-mingling is missed, the scurry
of hurrying people and the lost tempo
of traffic – the rhythms of urban life.
A dullness descends, unspoken grief
at a place, still and mute, that once cried

out for our notice, for caution in face
of a stealthy foe, an illness creeping
on a cat's sly paws down our sidewalks
and up stairways and even across
lawns at our city's outer-most edge.

Paying little heed, we now pay a price
for our complacency, our nod of heads
at notions of sneaking death, as if we
could little comprehend the need
to rouse ourselves from quiet stupor.

So now the emptiness prevails, and
wails are all that can be heard, and sighs
that waft down among the shadows
from balconies and rooftops of a city
that has gathered itself inside, alone.

Marjie Giffin lives in Indianapolis and has authored four regional histories. Her poetry recently appeared in *Snapdragon, Poetry Quarterly, Flying Island, The Kurt Vonnegut Literary Journal, The Saint Katherine Review, The Northwest Indiana Literary Journal, Through the Sycamores,* and *The Blue Heron Review.* One of her plays was produced in the IndyFringe Short Play Festival. Marjie is active in the Indiana Writers' Center and has taught both college writing and gifted education.

Editor

Barry Harris is editor of the *Tipton Poetry Journal* and three anthologies by Brick Street Poetry: *Mapping the Muse: A Bicentennial Look at Indiana Poetry; Words and Other Wild Things* and *Cowboys & Cocktails:Poems from the True Grit Saloon.* He has published one poetry collection, *Something At The Center.*

Barry lives in Brownsburg, Indiana and is retired from Eli Lilly and Company. He is married and father of two grown sons.

His poetry has appeared in *Kentucky Review, Valparaiso Poetry Review, Grey Sparrow, Silk Road Review, Saint Ann's Review, Boston Literary Magazine, Night Train, Silver Birch Press, Flying Island, Awaken Consciousness, Writers' Bloc,* and *Red-Headed Stepchild.* One of his poems was on display at the National Museum of Sport and another is painted on a barn in Boone County, Indiana as part of Brick Street Poetry's Word Hunger public art project. His poems are also included in these anthologies: *From the Edge of the Prairie; Motif 3: All the Livelong Day;* and *Twin Muses: Art and Poetry.*

He graduated a long time ago with a major in English from Ball State University.

Contributor Biographies

Duane Anderson currently lives in La Vista, Nebraska, and volunteers with a non-profit organization as a Donor Ambassador on their blood drives. He has had poems published in *The Pangolin Review, Fine Lines, The Sea Letter, Cholla Needles, Tipton Poetry Journal, Adelaide Literary Magazine* and several other publications.

Glen Armstrong holds an MFA in English from the University of Massachusetts, Amherst and teaches writing at Oakland University in Rochester, Michigan. He edits a poetry journal called *Cruel Garters* and has two current books of poems: *Invisible Histories* and *The New Vaudeville*. His work has appeared in *Poetry Northwest, Conduit,* and *Cream City Review*.

Hadley Austin is a Chicago based writer and filmmaker making a documentary about the legacy of uranium mining on the Navajo Nation.

Jan Ball started seriously writing poetry and submitting it for publication in 1998. Since then, she has had 309 poems accepted or published in the U.S., Australia, Canada, India, Ireland, Czech Republic and England. Published poems have appeared in: *ABZ, Atlanta Review, Calyx, Chiron, Main Street Rag, Phoebe* and many other journals. Her two chapbooks, *Accompanying Spouse* (2011) and *Chapter of Faults* (2014), have both been published by Finishing Line Press as well as Jan's first full length poetry collection, *I Wanted To Dance With My Father* (2017). Jan is a member of The Poetry Club of Chicago. She lived in Australia for fifteen years with her Australian husband, Ray Ball. Her two children, Geoffrey and Quentin, were born in Brisbane. Jan now lives in Chicago.

Blair Benjamin's poetry has appeared or is forthcoming in *The Threepenny Review, Lumina, Spillway,* and *Typehouse*. He is the Director of the Studios at MASS MoCA residency program for artists and writers in North Adams, Massachusetts.

Mary Birnbaum was born, raised, and educated in New York City. She has studied poetry at the Joiner Institute in UMass, Boston. Mary's translation of the Haitian poet Felix Morisseau-Leroy has been published in the *Massachusetts Review*, the anthology *Into English* (Graywolf Press), and will be in the 60 year anniversary anthology of the *Massachusetts Review* as well. Her work is forthcoming or has recently appeared in *I-70 Review,* the *J Journal,* and *Nixes Mate Review*.

Michael Brockley is a retired school psychologist who lives in Muncie, Indiana. His poems have appeared in *Atticus Review, Third Wednesday,* and *Jokes Review*. Poems are forthcoming in *Hobo Camp Review, Live Nude Poems,* and *Indianapolis Anthology*.

Michael Chang (they/them) is the proud recipient of a Brooklyn Poets fellowship. They were invited to attend the *Kenyon Review* Writers Workshop at Kenyon College as well as the Omnidawn Poetry Writing Conference at Saint Mary's College of California. Their writing has been published or is forthcoming in *The Minnesota Review, Yellow Medicine Review, Heavy Feather Review, UCityReview, Love's Executive Order, Glass Mountain, Thin Air, ellipsis… literature & art, Q/A Poetry, Yes Poetry, Typo Mag, Wrath-Bearing Tree, Bending Genres, The Hunger, Cabildo Quarterly, Willawaw Journal, Neon Garder, The Conglomerate, Queen Mob's Tea House, Funny Looking Dog Quarterly, London Grip, Rogue Agent, Kissing Dynamite, BULL Fiction, Literary Orphans, Animal: A Beast of a Literary Magazine, Collective Unrest, Pink Plastic House, Little Rose, Milk + Beans, Squawk Back*, and many others. Michael lives in New Jersey.

J.P. Check is a writer and illustrator from rural North Alabama. His poetry and paintings are influenced by his hometown and the South at large.

Douglas Cole has published six collections of poetry and a novella. His work has appeared in several anthologies as well as *The Chicago Quarterly Review, The Galway Review, Bitter Oleander, Louisiana Literature* and *Slipstream*. He has been nominated twice for a Pushcart and Best of the Net and received the Leslie Hunt Memorial Prize in Poetry. He lives and teaches in Seattle. His website is douglastcole.com.

Rosaleen Crowley was in born in Cork, Ireland and graduated from University College Cork. She relocated to Carmel, Indiana, in 1990. Along with images of water, nature and open spaces, themes of home, love, conflict, loss and isolation are looked at through her poetry. Her third book in her trilogy, *Point of Perception* will be published later this year.

Richard Dinges, Jr. lives in Nebraska, has an MA in literary studies from University of Iowa, and no longer manages information systems at an insurance company. *Green Hills Literary Lantern, Westview, Pinyon, Writers Bloc*, and *Big Windows Review* most recently accepted his poems for their publications.

Nathaniel Dolton-Thornton's poems have appeared or are forthcoming in *Tin House, Prelude, Poetry Salzburg Review, Griffith Review, Sycamore Review, TAB, The Account, Raritan*, and other publications. He studies political ecology as a Marshall Scholar at the University of Cambridge.

Renee Emerson was born in Tennessee and resides in Missouri. She has published poems in magazines such as *Perspectives, Still*, and *Valley Voices*, and currently teaches online courses for various universities. She is the author of *Keeping Me Still* (Winter Goose Publishing 2014) and *Threshing Floor* (Jacar Press 2016), and is online at www.ReneeEmerson.wordpress.com

Patrick Theron Erickson, a resident of Garland, Texas is a retired parish pastor put out to pasture himself. His work has appeared in *Tipton Poetry Journal, Grey Sparrow Journal*, and *The Main Street Rag*, among other publications, and more recently in *Torrid Literature Journal, South Florida Poetry Journal, Arlington Literary Journal* and *Sheila-Na-Gig*.

Marjie Giffin lives in Indianapolis and has authored four regional histories. Her poetry recently appeared in *Snapdragon, Poetry Quarterly, Flying Island, The Kurt Vonnegut Literary Journal, The Saint Katherine Review, The Northwest Indiana Literary Journal, Through the Sycamores,* and *The Blue Heron Review*. One of her plays was produced in the IndyFringe Short Play Festival. Marjie is active in the Indiana Writers' Center and has taught both college writing and gifted education.

James Green has worked as a naval officer, deputy sheriff, high school English teacher, professor of education, and administrator in both public schools and universities. Recipient of two Fulbright grants, he has served as a visiting scholar at the University of Limerick in Ireland and the National Chung Cheng University in Taiwan. In addition to academic publications, including three books, Green is the author of three chapbooks of poetry and a fourth, *Long Journey Home*, is forthcoming after winning the Charles Dickson Chapbook Contest sponsored by the Georgia Poetry Society., Individual poems have appeared in literary magazines in England, Ireland, and the United States. He resides in Muncie, Indiana.

Lois Marie Harrod's latest collection *Woman* was published by Blue Lyra in February 2020. Her *Nightmares of the Minor Poet* appeared in June 2016 from Five Oaks; her chapbook *And She Took the Heart* appeared in January 2016; *Fragments from the Biography of Nemesis* (Cherry Grove Press) and the chapbook *How Marlene Mae Longs for Truth* (Dancing Girl Press) appeared in 2013. A Dodge poet, she is published in literary journals and online ezines from *American Poetry Review* to *Zone 3*. She teaches at the Evergreen Forum in Princeton and at The College of New Jersey. Links to her online work: www.loismarieharrod.org

Following a B.A. from Williams College, **Bill Hollands** received a Dr. Herchel Smith Fellowship for two years of graduate work at Cambridge University, where he received his M.A. in English. He worked as a librarian for The New York Public Library and published a professional trade book, *Teaching the Internet to Library Staff and Users*. He is now a public high school English teacher in Seattle, where he lives with his husband and son. Poems are forthcoming in *Crosswinds* and *PageBoy*.

Fida Islaih is a self-published poet of seven collections and a freelance poetry editor living in Fishers, Indiana.

D. R. James has taught college writing, literature, and peace-making for 36 years and lives in the woods near Saugatuck, Michigan. His most recent of nine collections are *Flip Requiem* (Dos Madres Press, 2020), *Surreal Expulsion* (The Poetry Box, 2019), and *If god were gentle* (Dos Madres Press, 2017), and his micro-chapbook *All Her Jazz* is free, fun, and printable-for-folding at the Origami Poems Project.
https://www.amazon.com/author/drjamesauthorpage

F. X. James is the pseudonym for an oddball British expat hiding out in Minnesota. When not dissolving in another savage summer or fattening up for the next brutal winter, he's writing poems and stories on the backs of unpaid utility bills, and drinking too much dark ale. His words have appeared in many a magazine, and on a lucid day he can see all sorts of crazy things.

Tipton Poetry Journal – Spring 2020

Patrick Kalahar is a used & rare bookseller in Elwood, Indiana with his wife, poet and novelist Jenny. He is a book restorer, collector, and avid reader. His poems have appeared in anthologies published by Poets Unite Worldwide.

Casey Killingsworth has work in *The American Journal of Poetry, Kimera, Spindrift, Rain, Slightly West, Timberline Review, COG, Common Ground Review, Typehouse, Bangalore Review, Two Thirds North*, and other journals. His book of poems, *A Handbook for Water*, was published by Cranberry Press in 1995. As well he has a book on the poetry of Langston Hughes, *The Black and Blue Collar Blues* (VDM, 2008). Casey lives in Washington and has a Master's degree from Reed College.

Philip C. Kolin, the Distinguished Professor of English (Emeritus) at the University of Southern Mississippi and the Editor Emeritus of the *Southern Quarterly*, has published nine collections of poems, the most recent being *Reaching Forever* (Poems for the Poiema Poetry Series of Cascade Press, 2019). Kolin has also published extensively on Shakespeare and Tennessee Williams.

Former Indiana Poet Laureate **Norbert Krapf** is the author of thirteen poetry collections, including the recent *Indiana Hill Country Poems*. Forthcoming is *Southwest by Midwest*, which includes "Crazy Horse Is One." He is the winner of a Glick Indiana Author Award, a Creative Renewal Fellowship from the Arts Council of Indianapolis, and the Lucille Medwick Memorial Award from the Poetry Society of America. He collaborates with bluesman Gordon Bonham.

Having retired from teaching English and Communications, first in the US and for many years in Jamaica, **Mary Hills Kuck** now lives with her family in Massachusetts. She has received a Pushcart Prize Nomination and her poems have appeared in *Long River Run, Connecticut River Review, Hamden Chronicle, SIMUL: Lutheran Voices in Poetry, Caduceus, The Jamaica Observer, Fire Stick: A Collection of New & Established Caribbean Poets, Massachusetts State Poetry Society, Inc. Anthology*, the *Aurorean, Tipton Poetry Journal*, and others.

Bruce Levine, a 2019 Pushcart Prize Poetry Nominee, has spent his life as a writer of fiction and poetry and as a music and theatre professional. Over 300 of his works are published in over 25 on-line journals including *Ariel Chart, Friday Flash Fiction, Literary Yard;* over 30 print books including *Poetry Quarterly, Haiku Journal, Dual Coast Magazine*, and his shows have been produced in New York and around the country. Six eBooks are available from Amazon.com. His work is dedicated to the loving memory of his late wife, Lydia Franklin. He lives in New York with his dog, Daisy. Visit him at www.brucelevine.com.

Doris Lynch lives in Bloomington, Indiana and has recent work in *Flying Island, Frogpond, Modern Haiku, Contemporary Haibun Online, Drifting Sands Haibun* and in the anthologies: *Cowboys & Cocktails: Poetry from the True Grit Saloon* (Brick Street Poetry Inc., 2019), *Red River book of Haibun* (Red River Press, New Delhi, India, 2019), and *Another Trip Around the Sun: 365 Days of Haiku for Children Young and Old*, (Brooks Books, 2019).

Craig McVay, originally from West Lafayette, Indiana, has lived with his wife —and family nearby— in Columbus, Ohio for most of the past forty years. His degrees are in English and Classics, both of which he has taught in schools, community colleges and prisons in Maryland and Central Ohio; he currently is teaching mythology for Columbus State Community College. Co-ordinator of the longtime Columbus reading series, Peripatetic Poets, he has stories and poems in *Avatar Review, Blue Uniorn, Common Threads, Grey Sparrow, Icon* and others. A chapbook, *Joy in the Tomb of Hunting and Fishing*, will be published this spring or summer.

Karla Linn Merrifield has had 800+ poems appear in dozens of journals and anthologies. She has 14 books to her credit. Following her 2018 *Psyche's Scroll* (Poetry Box Select) is the new *Athabaskan Fractal: Poems of the Far North* from Cirque Press. She lives in Florida and is currently at work on a poetry collection, *My Body the Guitar*, inspired by famous guitarists and their guitars to be published by Before Your Quiet Eyes Holograph Series (Rochester, NY) in late 2021.

Daniel Edward Moore lives in Washington on Whidbey Island. He has poems forthcoming in *Weber Review, The Cape Rock, Kestrel, The Phoenix, Red Earth Review, RipRap, The Timberline Review, Capsule Stories, River Heron Review, Passages North,* and *Eastern Iowa Review*. He is the author of two chapbooks, *Confessions of a Pentecostal Buddhist* (CreateSpace) and *Boys* (Duck Lake Books). *Waxing the Dents*, a full length collection, is from Brick Road Poetry Press. Visit him at Danieledwardmoore.com.

James Mulhern lives in Florida and has published over seventy times in literary journals and anthologies. In 2015, Mr. Mulhern was awarded a fully paid writing fellowship to Oxford University in the United Kingdom. That same year, a story was longlisted for the Fish Short Story Prize. In 2017, he was nominated for a Pushcart Prize. His most recent novel, *Give Them Unquiet Dreams*, is a Readers' Favorite Book Award winner, a Notable Best Indie Book of 2019, and a Kirkus Reviews Best Book of 2019.

Lylanne Musselman is a native Hoosier and resides in Indianapolis. She teaches creative writing classes at Ivy Tech Community College in Indianapolis, and at the University of Indianapolis' School of Adult Learning. Lylanne is a regular contributor on WFHB radio's BloomingOUT with her story feature L WordS. An award winning poet, her poetry has appeared or is forthcoming in *Flying Island, New Voices News, Etchings, Tipton Poetry Journal, Poetry Motel*, and many *TallGrass Writers Guild Anthologies*.

Jessica Nguyen is a playwright, electronic musician, and writer living in Brooklyn. She has been published previously in *Tipton Poetry Journal, Open Thought Vortex, Sisyphus Quarterly, Crab Fat Magazine,* and *The Sex Letters Project*. She has also performed and written for The Boston Center for the Arts, The Living Gallery, Bindlestiff Studios, The Exponential Festival, and The Trans Theatre Festival.

Barry Peters lives in Durham and teaches in Raleigh, North Carolina. Publications include *The American Journal of Poetry, Best New Poets 2018, New Ohio Review, Poetry East* and *Rattle*.

Alex Pickens grew up in the Appalachian mountains between New England and Virginia. This year his poetry has been accepted by *Hawaii Pacific Review, Crab Orchard Review,* and *Constellations,* while last year his work was nominated for Best of the Net and a Pushcart Prize. He is the winner of *Appalachia journal's* 2019 Waterman Fund Essay Contest. Alex lives in North Carolina.

Timothy Pilgrim, Bellingham, Washington, a Pacific Northwest poet and 2018 Pushcart Prize nominee with several hundred acceptances by journals such as *Seattle Review, Cirque, San Pedro River Review, Toasted Cheese, Windsor Review, Hobart, Sleet Magazine* and *Third Wednesday,* is author of *Mapping water* (Flying Trout Press, 2016). See www.timothypilgrim.org for all his poetry.

William Pruitt is a writer, storyteller and assistant editor for *Narrative Magazine.* He has published poems in such places as *Ploughshares, Anderbo.com, Cottonwood, Country Journal, Ravensperch, Otis Nebula* and *Stoneboat*; in two chapbooks from White Pine and FootHills; and the self-published *Walking Home* from the Eastman House. His short stories appear in recent issues of *Indiana Voice Journal, Adelaide Literary Review, Oyster River Pages, Sick Lit, Crack the Spine Literary Magazine, Visitant, Midway* and *Hypertext*, and in an upcoming issue of *The Woven Tale Press*. William lives in Rochester, New York.

Donna Pucciani, a Chicago-based writer, has published poetry worldwide in such diverse publications as *Shi Chao Poetry, Istanbul Literary Review, Poetry Salzburg, The Pedestal,* and *Journal of Italian Translation.* Her most recent book of poems is *EDGES*.

Ron Riekki's books include *U.P.* (Ghost Road Press), *Posttraumatic* (Hoot 'n' Waddle), and *My Ancestors are Reindeer Herders and I Am Melting in Extinction* (Loyola University Maryland's Apprentice House Press). Riekki co-edited *Undocumented* (Michigan State University Press) and *The Many Lives of The Evil Dead* (McFarland), and edited *And Here* (MSU Press), *Here* (MSU Press, Independent Publisher Book Award), and *The Way North* (Wayne State University Press, Michigan Notable Book).

Timothy Robbins has been teaching English as a Second Language for 28 years. His poems have appeared in *Main Street Rag, Off The Coast, Bayou Magazine, Slant, Tipton Poetry Journal, Cholla Needles* and many others. He has published three volumes of poetry: *Three New Poets* (Hanging Loose Press), *Denny's Arbor Vitae* (Adelaide Books) and *Carrying Bodies* (Main Street Rag Press). He lives in Wisconsin with his husband of 22 years.

William Snyder, Jr. has published poems in *Atlanta Review, Poet Lore,* and *Southern Humanities Review* among others. He was the co-winner of the 2001 Grolier Poetry Prize; winner of the 2002 Kinloch Rivers Chapbook competition; The CONSEQUENCE Prize in Poetry, 2013; the 2015 Claire Keyes Poetry Prize; Tulip Tree Publishing Stories That Need To Be Told 2019 Merit Prize for Humor; and Encircle Publications 2019 Chapbook Contest. He lives in Fargo, North Dakota and teaches writing and literature at Concordia College in Moorhead, Minnesota.

Canadian poet, fiction writer, and playwright **J. J. Steinfeld** lives on Prince Edward Island, where he is patiently waiting for Godot's arrival and a phone call from Kafka. While waiting, he has published 20 books, including *Identity Dreams and Memory Sounds* (Poetry, Ekstasis Editions, 2014), *Madhouses in Heaven, Castles in Hell* (Stories, Ekstasis Editions, 2015), *An Unauthorized Biography of Being* (Stories, Ekstasis Editions, 2016), *Absurdity, Woe Is Me, Glory Be* (Poetry, Guernica Editions, 2017), *A Visit to the Kafka Café* (Poetry, Ekstasis Editions, 2018), and *Gregor Samsa Was Never in The Beatles* (Stories, Ekstasis Editions, 2019). His short stories and poems have appeared in numerous periodicals and anthologies internationally, and over 50 of his one-act plays and a handful of full-length plays have been performed in Canada and the United States.

Wally Swist's books include *Huang Po and the Dimensions of Love* (Southern Illinois University Press, 2012), selected by Yusef Komunyakaa as co-winner in the 2011 Crab Orchard Series Open Poetry Contest, and *A Bird Who Seems to Know Me: Poems Regarding Birds & Nature* (Ex Ophidia Press, 2019), the winner of the 2018 Ex Ophidia Press Poetry Prize. His recent poems have or will appear in *Commonweal*, *Rattle*, and *Transference: A Literary Journal Featuring the Art & Process of Translation*. Recent books include *The Bees of the Invisible* (2019) and *Evanescence: Selected Poems* (2020), both with Shanti Arts. He currently lives in Massachusetts.

Anannya Uberoi is a full-time software engineer and part-time tea connoisseur based in Madrid, Spain. Her poems and short stories have appeared or are forthcoming in *Jaggery*, *LandLocked*, *Deep Wild*, *Lapiz Lazuli*, and *eFiction India*. Her writing has also been featured on *The Delhi Walla* and *The Dewdrop*, among other literary blogs.

Mark Vogel lives at the back of a Blue Ridge holler with his wife, Susan Weinberg, an accomplished fiction and creative non-fiction writer, and two foster sons. He currently serves as Professor of English at Appalachian State University in Boone, North Carolina, where he co-directs the English Education Program. Poems and short stories have appeared in several dozen literary journals.

Vivian Wagner is an associate professor of English at Muskingum University in New Concord, Ohio. Her essays and poems have appeared in *Slice Magazine, Muse/A Journal, Forage Poetry Journal, Pittsburgh Poetry Review, McSweeney's Internet Tendency, Gone Lawn, The Atlantic, Narratively, The Ilanot Review, Silk Road Review, Zone 3*, and other publications. She's the author of a memoir, *Fiddle: One Woman, Four Strings, and 8,000 Miles of Music* (Citadel-Kensington); a full-length poetry collection, *Raising* (Clare Songbirds Publishing House); and three poetry chapbooks: *The Village* (Aldrich Press-Kelsay Books), *Making* (Origami Poems Project), and *Curiosities* (Unsolicited Press).

Gabriel Welsch writes fiction and poetry and is the author of four collection of poems, the most recent of which is *The Four Horsepersons of a Disappointing Apocalypse* (Steel Toe Books, 2013). His work appears recently or will appear in *Ploughshares, Asheville Poetry Review, Atticus Review, Lake Effect, Bodega Magazine, Bluestem, Pembroke Review,* and *trampset*. He lives in Pittsburgh with his family, and works as vice president of marketing and communications at Duquesne University.

Danielle Wong lives in Quebec and is the author of *Bubble Fusion*, a collection of poems about raising a child with autism. Her other work has appeared in *Soft Cartel, Montreal Writes, Patterns*, and other anthologies. She enjoys losing herself in forests, but can be found at https://www.daniellewong.ca.

Made in the USA
Middletown, DE
07 July 2020